Jim Emerton

COUNTRYMAN

Tales from field, marsh and woodland

Jim Emerton

COUNTRYMAN

Tales from field, marsh and woodland

MEREO
Cirencester

Mereo Books

1A The Wool Market Dyer Street Cirencester Gloucestershire GL7 2PR
An imprint of Memoirs Publishing www.mereobooks.com

COUNTRYMAN: 978-1-86151-762-3

First published in Great Britain in 2016
by Mereo Books, an imprint of Memoirs Publishing

The address for Memoirs Publishing Group Limited can be found at
www.memoirspublishing.com

The Memoirs Publishing Group Ltd Reg. No. 7834348

The Memoirs Publishing Group supports both The Forest Stewardship Council®
(FSC®) and the PEFC® leading international forest-certification organisations. Our
books carrying both the FSC label and the PEFC® and are printed on FSC®-certified
paper. FSC® is the only forest-certification scheme supported by the leading
environmental organisations including Greenpeace. Our paper procurement policy
can be found at www.memoirspublishing.com/environment

Typeset in 12/20pt Century Schoolbook
by Wiltshire Associates Publisher Services Ltd. Printed and bound in Great Britain
by Marston Book Services Ltd, Oxfordshire

CONTENTS

COUNTRY BOY

I love to be where the wild goose flies across lonely skies
Morning mist and the sparkling dew
in fields where a simple few feel the power of the awakening sun.

The cock crows as the day comes alive to the orchestra of nature.
In far green pastures, pheasants preen like beauty queens,
unaware of the wily old fox
as it engages in the dance of death
and pounces on an unsuspecting vole,
whose concealment in the long grass cannot save it.

Far from the pulse of city man
I flow with the wind and the tide,
intoxicated by freedom.
This is my hour, my day at home in the heart of nature,
where the butterfly caresses the air with ethereal emerald wings
where the skylark sings one more sweet note
to all that is good and beautiful in the cradle of life.

Introduction

I love writing. There are some beautiful minds who have left lasting imprints in books, and I long to follow their example. It makes me happy that my work has been read in various parts of the world as a result of my study and dedication and any inbuilt talents I may have. When my body turns to dust and atoms, I hope some of my work will still be a source of interest, somewhere in the world.

I was born in the Nightingale Home in Derby before moving to Skegness, Lincolnshire, when I was a small boy. My father, a cool, kind and gentle man, introduced me to pigeons when I was three years old. Although a quiet, socially inept and deeply sensitive boy, I was instantly hooked and fascinated by the gentle beauty of Charlie Fantail and other lovely fancy pigeons and crossbred birds.

Before long we had bought some brightly-coloured tumblers, and my formative years were spent gazing into the sky at the acrobats of the pigeon world. Soon, at Skegness, I became aware of stray racing pigeons, and with stealth and cunning I caught many a one. The first stray I saw, at around the age of five, was a pencil-blue young bird, complete with race rubber. In the early years I developed a love of all things natural and was later to graduate from the Royal Botanic Gardens, Kew, and qualify to teach Rural Studies at the University of Birmingham's Worcester College.

Some time after my sixth birthday we moved to the Lincolnshire Wolds to run the post office at Skendleby. We had three acres of grass paddock and orchard there and I spent five happy years gazing at my roller pigeons and walking the woods and hedgerows. From this time on, everywhere we travelled I caught stray racers and kept them in the house loft. I was always out and disappearing, serving my apprenticeship in nature. Having said that, I was also a cruel, ruthless boy who, like many other country boys, took up shooting, and later I became a good rough shot and wildfowler.

Although quiet and polite, I was cheeky enough to knock at people's doors and charm my way to catch roosting strays on their windowsills. (I still call on people today to see their birds and I am normally welcomed due to my cheeky self-confidence.)

At the age of eleven we moved back to Derbyshire, settling in Alvaston, and managed to settle the good red roller cock and some other chosen birds. My teenage years were spent cultivating my Birmingham Roller team, whilst enduring the strict teaching regime at Spondon Park Grammar School. I would rush home from school to watch my rollers perform, a habit which enabled me to develop intense observational skills, although it got a little out of hand because I would not do the homework the academics demanded. I got to know the roller men, the tippler men and the racing men of Derby. Jack Whitehouse, now in his 80s, is still a big name today. Also developing fast was my competitive and perfectionist attitude and I always tried to do my best, an attitude which was cultivated by my strict and no-nonsense upbringing. My father had been an army sergeant, but I could beat him at arm-wrestling at 12 years of age.

In Derby city centre were the riverside gardens, and there I would sit like an old recidivist and catch strays with peanuts. I recall good old Pigeon Percy, a colourful and well-known character. Catching the wiliest of old racer strays, I would put them in a battered fishing creel and return home to Alvaston — an electric ride on a trolley bus. Soon, since I excelled in my chosen horticulture, I was sent to Askham Bryan College for two years for advanced study, and had to part with some newly-acquired racing pigeons.

I confess to having become an institutionalised

and professional student, spending a further three years at the Royal Botanics, Kew, and a further year at Teacher Training College, studying for 11 years in total. What an incredible amount of hard work it was. You see, I had a very greedy intellect and thirst for knowledge. All this has been worthwhile, since I am able to express my inner core in print. My study years were punctuated by pigeons, like the time I hand-reared a baby woodpigeon taken from the trees at Askham Bryan College at night. Then there was the racing pigeon I kept as a pet in my wardrobe in my digs (out of sight of my landlord).

In 1976 1 started with racing birds at Sycamore Cottage, Holtby, York. The development of my strain and my racing activities have been well documented on websites and in magazines. I enjoy my life today now that the sweat of my brow has borne fruit.

Country Life and
Country People

I recall my childhood in Skendleby in the Lincolnshire Wolds with love and sweet nostalgia. There we had a menagerie covering three acres, where I was surrounded by and immersed in wildlife. Wild geese grazed our paddock, and I indulged in early initiations into field sports with the sons of the Crust family of farmers, using catapults, .410 shotguns and air rifles and ratting with terriers, hard-bitten little rascals. We lived as a feral bunch of lads, climbing trees and collecting birds' eggs in boxes of sawdust, and, and I loved it all.

When I was older and married, my passion for the countryside and all things wild continued. My wife Jean and I loved game fairs, country shows, terrier or lurcher shows and often used to enjoy going to them.

A pair of young rogues

John Shinn and I met in 1960 as new boys at

Spondon Park Grammar School, Derby. We became well known for making rude noises, particularly in English and Geography. This must have impressed our teacher Bill Cunningham, because he gave me a lowly grade G for English and my report read 'Insolent and a thorough nuisance in class, especially in English Literature'. Now John was good at English Grammar and I gained inspiration from sitting next to him. John is a big, strong, rugged fellow and his dad supplied me with a twelve-bore shotgun and a .22 rifle. We grew up together playing for the school rugby team and rough shooting, which I loved.

Through John's influence – he was the mature one – we stayed in the houseboat with Kenzie Thorpe, the 'Wild Goose Man', on the Wash saltings. More of Kenzie later. We were two adventurous outdoor sorts together. Sometimes John would watch my Rollers, but he was more interested in pigeon shooting. Nowadays John is a first-class all round shot and engineer, and his affinity with working Labradors and spaniels has to be seen to be believed. He is a regular character on the shooting scene with the rich and famous, including Michael Massarella, and recently loaded for Liz Hurley. He can perhaps be best described as a hard case with a soft centre and is a definite one-off. A book of his would be a best seller.

Fish and fishing

In 1954, when I was five, Mum took little me in short trousers fishing for tiddlers in a local pond at Skegness. I recall my first sight of those little silver sticklebacks dangling from the worm. Although I was never a great angler, I did enjoy my adventures near water, from Lincolnshire to the Florida Everglades.

In the 1960s we had great fun pulling gudgeon out of a local stream at Alvaston, another chapter in the small boy's dream. I tried for the eels in the dykes of the Wash over many hours, and zero was the result. One day a gang of us grammar school boys descended on Locko Park lake at Spondon, Derbyshire. We pulled out nets of lovely striped, bristling perch to the sight and sound of grebes and coots and dragonflies that dazzled in the summer air. It was such a perfect day, and all part of the young boy's adventure.

In 1962 my family stayed in a chalet in North Wales. In the grounds was a shallow trout stream, where I managed to bag some trout and eels on a night line baited with cockles. Later I would go out with a professional fisherman on the Conway estuary. We baited our lines with soft-back crab and pulled out juicy dabs and flounders and hooked a big turbot. Fried in gentle fat, the fish were beautiful to eat.

One day while he was casting into the sea my poor old dad Jim hooked himself in the face, and as stoical as he was I teased the big sea hook from his cheek.

One day in the 1960s my father and I went to the big lakes at Kedleston Hall, Derbyshire. We spotted the primeval lamprey, a parasitic but fascinating species. The men would use dead and live bait for pike while we pursued roach and silver bream and other coarse species. I was never to become an expert fisherman, but I enjoyed moderate successes with memorable days in wild and beautiful habitats. Angling takes great practical skill and intuitive awareness of nature.

My love of the natural world, an adventurous spirit and energy, saw me angling as far away as the Everglades. From the back of a pulsating V8 airboat we fed marshmallows to hungry alligators, and in pure delight I pulled out my first fish. From minnows to tommy ruffs, stone loaches and bullheads I did enjoy the sport.

Later I would watch the fox hunts at Holtby near York. The killing of the fox by a hound pack is now banned of course. The hunt is primal and instinctual and may be perceived as cruel by sensitive, thoughtful and compassionate people, as may any pursuit where sentient lifeforms are exploited for gratification.

Sometimes the hounds would come into my garden. Working beagles are nice dogs to see, yet running to brown hares is banned, and they are in decline due to intensive farming, poaching, hunting and loss of optimal habitat.

Cocker's fighting cock

From time to time you meet people of great spiritual individuality, and I have encountered some wonderful characters on my travels, from Alvaston to Afghanistan. I have known country people who were in intimate contact with the pulse of life and the ways of nature, and have inspired me to poetry.

At Holtby along the lanes of Yorkshire, I encountered a remarkable family of Romanies. Old Montagu Cocker Smith came walking along with his piebald horses and his bowtop caravan. Over the years we traded chat around the campfire smoking his Condor twist, and we gave them butter and cheese and a few racing pigeons as friendly gestures. I was impressed by their free-spirited individualism, cultural traditions and ancient lifestyle. They lived in the bosom of nature, a hardy, spartan way of being, and knew the meaning of sun, wind, snow and rain.

One day 'Cocker' asked me to overwinter his old English game fighting cock to me for a while, a black and white bird of great spirit and the finest bird I ever looked in the eye. I put him in to join my other birds and he despatched my banty cock in double quick time. When I let the beast out he flew from tree to tree, crowing loudly. Then he sat on the cottage roof to announce his considerable presence to all of nature as well as the human community. Mother said 'Either you go or the cockerel does, which will it be?' So he had to go. Of course cock fighting is illegal in the UK, and is widely regarded as barbaric, although it is the national sport of the Philippines. Nevertheless the old cock was the embodiment of pure spirit, an awesome creature of fiery and noble beauty.

Creatures of
the Wild

The Living God

Nature is the living god
It forms us, shapes us, takes us
There is no start, no finish
Its power will never diminish
Wise man does not bother
He knows his centre, the Earth Mother
The death of a spider, firefly burned
The great wheel of life is always turned.

Birds of prey

I love to see the windhover or kestrel poised in the air currents and ready to pounce on a field vole. Birds of prey of all kinds awaken the instincts of man, and birders find them fascinating on a primitive and profound level of stimulation. From the humble kestrel to the dominant goshawk and the murderous peregrine, pigeon fanciers may be at the mercy of them in many parts of the world. With marauding hen sparrowhawks frequently hitting my racers, I had to live with them for very many years, and on the open loft system. As a naturalist I tried to adopt a realistic approach to my birds' place in nature and that of myself.

The essence of a performance racing pigeon is in its navigation, will, desire and physique, which enable it to fly home under the pressures of the natural environment, coping with all the difficult conditions it must face in up to 1000 miles of homing. Race reality produces the rare great one.

The Artic Tern eclipses all that pigeons can do in terms of flight migration.

Hunting with birds

Hunting with raptors is an ancient outdoor pursuit associated with the nobility and with a strict hierarchy – a goshawk for a yeoman, a kestrel for a knave, an eagle for an emperor. I have great sympathy for my fellow pigeon fanciers as female sparrowhawks and peregrine falcons are ruthless predators of racers, rollers and tipplers. A hen sparrowhawk will down a pigeon by your feet. If undisturbed she will mantle the bird, stripping and eating the flesh while the pigeon is still alive. They are awesome ambush predators when fattening up to lay in late winter and early spring. This is raw nature and part of the tooth-and-claw syndrome, if you consider that man is part of the natural world. Hawks and falcons are majestic, beautiful birds, but their numbers are sometimes out of balance with other bird species in an ecosystem.

Nick, an old friend, and I once took a hen buzzard out rabbiting, and it was wonderful to see her gliding along with deceptive speed.

In my worldly travels I have watched hunting birds in Africa, Europe and Asia. The Sahara is magical in the moonlight and twilight and you can listen to the desert sands as they whisper ancient secrets. I am in awe of the wonders of the Earth.

My abiding memories are of eagles soaring over the Himalaya and the elegant condors over the Andes. Falconry displays featuring Harris Hawks and Gyrfalcons are good educational tools. I do urge young people to switch off their mobiles sometimes and take a walk on the wild side. The wild places of the world have taught me all the important things I know about the natural elements and life and of death.

Eagles and kingfishers

When I stayed in a Victorian houseboat on Lake Dahl in Kashmir, I watched eagles soaring on high thermals over the Himalaya, and fish glistening in the lake below. I was delighted to spot four species of kingfisher, the jewels of the avian world. The pied variety was nice, yet I was transfixed by the emerald green of the exotic malachite kingfisher. If heaven be in your mind, then you may feel it out in the big outdoors.

In 1979 when walking through the ancient ruins of Ephesus, we saw the sky lit up by the aerial acrobatics of a wonderful bird – the roller or blue jay. What an honour to see these creatures in full glow.

Wonders of the avian world

In 1955 my father Jim bought some lovely Birmingham Roller pigeons, having flown them as a young man himself. These were in rich colours with a dun and a red cock. In 1956 we moved from Skegness to Skendleby, where I spent many hours gazing up into the sky; my head has been in the clouds ever since. Now these birds are true wonders of the avian world as they spin backwards or sideways at great velocity.

I have met some of the great competition roller men in the world. The flying of these birds teaches silent meditation and fills the mind with abstract calm. We assume the trait is brain-based and inherited, and a kit of colourful rollers in a group spin is wonderful. The red cock died at Alvaston, Derby, having been flown out in three counties of England, and his red son was a tight and fast spinner. Thus my love of pigeons was born and remains to this day.

Teasels and goldfinches

In my garden are 9ft tall *Dipsacum*, Latin for teasel. I love to see the squabbling charms of goldfinches visiting them, and I have learned to sex them by eye. The seed-eating finches are great and I have spent hours watching redpolls and siskins on the alder seeds, quietly surviving as arboreal acrobats.

Birds of the saltings

The autumn flights over the Wash saltings are spectacular in their intensity, a bird lover's dream. Haunting curlew cries are beautiful sounds to receptive ears, while thousands of knots swirl in flocks to evade predation by peregrines. Whooper swans wing by in majestic formation and marsh harriers patrol the stalk edges. Short-eared owls study you as they hover above your head. The ambience of nature generates the ultimate feelings of mysticism – you feel so alive and bursting with life, which settles you into a quiet euphoria. Paradise and heaven are to be found in nature.

Hobs, jills and bunnies

Ferrets can be furry, smooth creatures in the hand. I always treated them with respect as they will nip you, as Brian Plummer's did. It was exciting to stop a warren of rabbits with the purse nets and enter a nice polecat ferret hob. The bunnies would spring into the nets – and they do make a lovely casserole of lean protein food with country vegetables and gravy.

One day Dave and Mick and I netted an old warren at Lower Marishes near Pickering, Yorkshire. The argument is the control of pests and the balance of nature, yet many do it for sport, and to satiate deeply-held instincts. Men, in particular, can be compelled to kill.

The warren was so deep that I volunteered to be lowered into it head first as my feet were held. In the dark and feeling forward, I pulled out five live bunnies one by one, and was then pulled out back into the light of day. It was one of those mad, legendary days out in the wilds.

In the winter snows Mick and I went in pursuit of old conies. In the biting wind we heard the distress call of a rabbit. Mick shot off in his wellies like shit off a stick. Amazingly he came back with a live rabbit in his hands with a big old stoat clinging to its neck. Now feral ferrets can be found in the wild, yet I see many a stoat and weasel, and they inhabited my cottage garden. They are truly magical, athletic creatures to behold, especially profiled against the snow.

Jackdaws are hardy, clever corvids birds that may live for 30 years. They form colonies in which there is a distinct hierarchical relationship in the pecking order from top to bottom. I admire them for their wily intelligence and survival cunning. The mate of the king jackie becomes the queen, and so on right down to the pariah birds below.

At Skendleby they used to nest in the chimney pot of our outhouse, and there were dozens nesting in the jackie trees. These were ancient elms in a grove where the Cruft children, Lynda, Giles, George and I would examine the eggs by climbing up a web of witches' brooms.

We feed foxes, woodpigeons, magpies and crows as well as jackdaws in the garden, as I like their company. Each year the young of the local corvids willingly take our offerings. Crows and ravens are associated with the shadows of men who indulge in the occult. The corvids as a group are true survivors with their cunning and adaptability, and their descendants will surely be among the last life-forms on the Earth, long after man has gone.

A fox in the garden

An encounter with a red fox was instrumental in persuading me to hang up my gun. In a field hedgerow in Chellaston, Derbyshire, he faced me and I knew that I must not shoot. I realised in those intense moments that we were all united in nature, all joint life forms on Planet Earth. The fox in its dance is a mesmerising sight, so graceful and beautiful. The prey may be a grasshopper, a vole or a rabbit. Foxes, led by hungry vixens, forage on carcasses in my garden, and I have been observing them in gardens since 1963. Every facet of cunning ad near-human intelligence is demonstrated by old Reynard. I love the way they survive and lope along so confidently in close proximity to humans.

My garden is a little ecosystem that has matured into a hotspot of nature. Nature abhors a straight line, and the untidiness of my garden is its friend. Apart from man our foxes are the kings of the little jungle. My conservation conscience has kicked in.

A fox is poised with cunning intent
The vole's last breath will soon be spent
Old Reynard coils in deathly dance
This was the creature's final chance
The circle of life is made complete
By Mother Nature's will they meet.

The wolf

Arctic and timber wolves are my favourite lupine creatures. Persecuted by man, they have survived since long before the dawn of humanity, and will continue to do so if we let them. With a human population explosion it would be wonderful to see the expansion of suitable habitat. A howling wolf alone on a rock in the moonlight is an archetypal symbol of wilderness, freedom and primal instinct, and I love the concept.

Lone wolf howling in the night
Under the moon and the stars' cold light
Maligned by man, nature's savage
A lonely deer he will surely ravage
Fiend or devil, his spirit lives on
He flows with the wind, the earth, the sun.

With Ben and the bag

A goose falls to Jim's gun

Accepting a retrieve from Ben

With Ben

Taking a shot from the
gangplank

Jim on the gangplank with a
curlew

Three duck and a goose down

Kenzie Thorpe by the houseboat

Kenzie in the famous houseboat

The houseboat festooned with quarry after a
successful morning's shoot

Feeding tame geese

Jim the hippy in India

Snake charmer
in India

Cooneen Jane, the greyhound

Shooting Man

Wilderness

Ice crystals cling to my face
The foaming tide, fluffed with salt
Creeps around my feet
Seals calling from lonely sandbanks
Of the North Sea washes
An eerie, plaintive curlew cry
The sound resonating with each tingling sensation
At one with ancient and eternal elements.

The snowflakes, driven by Arctic wind
Burn my face with a sweet embrace
Alone in my uniqueness
Tasting the joy of nature's freedom
Urged on by primal instincts
Into heady and sublime euphoria
The purity of spirit
United at last.

A man at large in the wild

The atmosphere in the wild places of the world when you are out there as a hunter is truly magical. I would often go out in the night with a .410 to stalk rabbits on local allotments at Alvaston. Silence and stealth are your friends in this kind of hunting, as the range of a .410 is not great. Rabbit stew with dumplings is delicious, but not as delicious as the exhilaration of the chase. Out in nature you feel naked, raw and full of life. For a nature boy like me, the feeling smacks of reality and personal truth. Now in my years of quiet reflection the past looms large, with its memories of times when the spirit was wild, unfettered and free. I spend my days walking out in the morning dew and giving thanks to the rain that falls and the sun that shines, and for the joys of being a man in the cosmos at large.

Pigeons in the park

In 1965 I started work as a garden boy apprentice on Derby Parks and was paid £3 for a 44-hour week. The location was the scenic and lovely Darley Abbey Park. At this stage I was absorbed by the wild and instinctual outdoor elements of shooting. The respected and feared John Graham, head gardener, gave me permission to fire a 12-bore before the park opened in the morning. My quarry were crows, woodpigeons, stock doves and grey squirrels, which I spotted in the huge old beech trees of the woods. It was outrageous walking at times with a black Labrador.

On one occasion an echo from my shots alerted the security man, who seemed happy to take a woodpigeon from my bag. I would not dream of doing such a thing today, in my mellow age, as it seems both archaic and anachronistic. As a parks worker I accounted for some nice tasty rabbits at Alvaston Lake too.

Early guns

In the 1950s at Skendleby I started with a Diana Model 16 that fired darts and a Milbro catapult, and I was a mean stone thrower. By the 1960s I had a Webley Falcon .22 air rifle, a BSA Airsporter .22 air rifle and a BSA .410 bolt-action shotgun. A retired policeman fitted me out with a Remington .22 repeating hunting rifle. The mainstay gun I used for rough shooting and wildfowling was a cheap Spanish Ligano Herald Mark 2 twelve bore. It was heavily choked and accounted for everything from snipe to wild geese. Kenzie Thorpe said I was the best young shot on pigeon to have gone out with him.

The 12 bore and the Airsporter were eventually given to my friend Maurice Shinn's son John, and the Remington was surrendered to the police. Maurice was a shrewd and amiable fellow and an inveterate poacher. My instincts had been very sharp and quick with all the guns. Out with dog and gun, solo, you learn about yourself and to respect nature in all its forms. It is the ancient predator in the psyche of man that makes him hunt – I realise this now, in my wiser years.

Alvaston was a nice smallholding where lovely old Ted Fearns tended his crops and orchards. John had a BSA Meteor and I my Webley Falcon. As young rascals we shot the starlings that feasted on the pears and plums, hard-case country lads enjoying the sport. House sparrows were legitimate quarry in those days and I regret that we accounted for some of those in the old chicken runs.

It would be an encounter with a beautiful fox that mesmerised me and led to my parting with the guns, although I had to dispose of the rats that haunted my pigeon racing days. Here the BSA Airsporter came in handy. In the mid-sixties I recall ratting at Chellaston, where a council tip was crawling with crickets and cockroaches. It was disgusting, an experience, only beaten by culling rats in a knacker's yard. That was deeply offensive, yet memorable. My grandfather Tom crushed one to death as it climbed up his baggy trousers, and the story became a family legend. Rats are intelligent creatures and great survivors. Although they dwell in places that men despise, I have a sneaking admiration for them.

Rough shooting adventures

One morning, in pursuit of shooting rights, I jumped on my Claude Butler racing bike at 32 Gilbert Street, Alvaston, and headed off down Shardlow Road, calling at every farm on the way. It was another exercise in my usual persistence, and it took me as far as a village called Wilson in Leicestershire. Here a kindly farmer gave me express permission to shoot over 300 acres of fields, hedgerows, railway line and copse. I was in rough shooting heaven, and walked the land regularly with my side-by-side 12 bore with full and half-choke barrels.

In those days coveys of English partridges paused to grit on the disused railway line, which made good habitat for them. They were excellent shooting and good eating, along with the wily old cock pheasants, rabbits, hares and the odd duck. In those days I went with a .22 rifle slung over my shoulder for attempts at bagging long-range quarry – rather macho at the time. My excursions into rough shooting continued on Askham Bryan College estate as a horticultural student from 1967 to 69. The gun was kept in room 31 with a bandolier of live cartridges. By this time I had become a good, sharp shot, yet always safe. It was a bit archaic to gut hares in my room, with a pet crow sitting on the window sill. The tutor on the shoot was my lecturer, Mr Boydell, a nice chap.

Out at dawn with dog and gun

It seems a paradox that a young man should want to take the lives of beautiful birds and animals, but it is based on deep-rooted instincts. As a country boy in Lincolnshire, Derbyshire and Yorkshire, I was driven by the deeply instinctual, primal urge of the hunter. I was in my element out in the wind, rain and snow and sometimes under the moon at night. The thrill of the chase was both intoxicating and electrifying, and it was satisfying to a rugged and somewhat cruel young man.

In days gone by I would get up and go at the crack of dawn with my Labrador Ben and walk the stubble fields, the woods and hedges to flush out pheasants, partridges, rabbits and hares and flight the woodpigeons coming into roost. The essence was sport, skill and developing into a good shot. My best on wild pigeons was 55 with just over 60 cartridges. It took place in a burdock hide, a spinney in Thorney, Cambridgeshire, with my old friend Kenzie the Wild Goose Man.

Alone in wilderness and down to your instincts, you may learn some serious lessons in life. Stripped of the veneer of society, you gain a sense of stark reality. As a wildfowler in the unforgiving Wash marshes, I embraced life, death and the wild elements and felt the wind, snow and rain on bare skin. A walk along the sea wall under the moon and stars is both eerie and enchanting. Every man should explore the freedom that the true primitive feels.

Kenzie, Hawkeye and the Boy

Let me tell you how I came to know the legendary Kenzie Thorpe. In 1965, my friend John Shinn responded to an advert in *Shooting Times & Country Magazine.* Kenzie was inviting people to stay on his boat and study seals and the Wash wildlife. I was eager to join my friend on this great adventure. We were driven down in an Austin Cambridge and out into the wilderness at the famous Shep White's, beyond the flat potato fields, the quaint village characters and an abundance of brown hares and pheasants. To crown it all it was raining heavily, so the trek across open creeks and saltings scattered our provisions all over the marsh.

Mackenzie Thorpe was an artist who had worked with Sir Peter Scott, an ex-jailbird, middleweight boxing champ, poacher and wildfowler par excellence. His eyes were deep with knowledge, his face craggy with wind and salt exposure. He was a unique and solitary figure in this bleak landscape.

Kenzie greeted us by snapping that we were late. He was a tough master. This was the start of two young boys' adventure game, as we roughed it out to the stalk edges, the sandbanks and the edge of the North Sea with the greatest wild goose man of all time. He called us Hawkeye (John) and the Boy (me). The sights and sounds and the atmosphere have shaped my life.

The saltings were a wild, rugged and remote wilderness of tidal creeks, sea lavender and samphire. At high spring tide the boat lifted on its moorings and you were floating on the edge of the North Sea. At times like this my imagination was fired and intensified – will the moorings break and the boat float out to the eternal sea?

Cooking the potatoes from the local fields was done on a paraffin stove with sea water scooped from the depths. A foggy cloud enveloped the boat and the calls of the common seals intensified in the murky dampness.

John and I embraced nature full on as we learned the Wash secrets; the hordes of waders, the ducks and geese, the marsh harriers floating by and the wily marsh pheasants as they tried to evade the gun. We lived the boy's adventure tale and these essential times by the sea, sun and stars framed my life and instincts forever. Old Kenzie passed away in 1976, after which, by Romany tradition, the houseboat was torched.

The dangers of the foreshore

Danger is endemic in many field sports, and many people lose their lives in the wild places of the world to the gun, the mountain, the sea and other natural hazards. In 1967 Kenzie and I encountered an uncharted danger zone in the tidal creeks of the Wash marshes. With a cat tide rising at a great rate, we were cut off by the fast-flowing muddy depths in a large artery. The old rogue saved my life that day, by feeling for a raised sandbank with his thigh wader which was good enough for me to risk following him to safety.

In 1967 Kenzie and I surveyed the high spring tide as it flooded in towards the sea wall at Shep White's on the Wash saltings. Old Kenzie proclaimed that there was one man in Lincolnshire who could reach the houseboat on foot in the rising cat tide. Now there is a challenge, I thought to myself. With fear and trepidation I followed the great man out, echoing his every crafty move as survival mode kicked in. After some anxiety and sweat we both reached the moored boat, and soon we were afloat on the inexorable tide.

Old Kenzie took many well-known people shooting, and I remember him taking the actor James Robertson Justice punt gunning. The old boy remains a great character in my nostalgic imagery. The Wash was the habitat of many eccentric hard cases and I loved them all.

Man versus mouse

Fourteen days on Kenzie's houseboat on the Wash saltings would heighten your senses and stimulate your imagination. Sometimes mice crawled along the bilges and ventured out at night on food sorties. Kenzie issued a challenge about one particular mouse – 'Bet you can't get 'im'. From then on, to conquer that little animal became an *idée fixe*, even an obsession.

That night before bunk time, I set the trap. It must not fail! Cheese tends to crumble into flakes, affording a safe meal for the raider, so I daubed the spike with butter. Then I extinguished the tilly lamp and waited, hardly daring to breathe or blink in the near blackness. The vast loneliness and emptiness of the marshes outside seemed to penetrate the woodwork of the boat.

The silence was broken by an erratic scraping;

the mouse had come to explore. Chewing and scratching ensued as our little invader raided the sugar bag, a damp and dirty store of near-solid sugar. Suddenly the scrapings stopped, to be followed by a loud twang – the trap had sprung! I flicked on the torch and collected my prize with great satisfaction. It is such simple pleasures that remain strong in the minds of men.

Rodents are fascinating animals, and none more so than the brown rat, despicable creature as it is and credited with every possible evil and malevolent power. The rat is the epitome of filth and despised by humans the world over. However there are those who credit it with the praiseworthy qualities of intelligence and cleanliness.

As I was sitting one night in my bunk on the houseboat after struggling to get to sleep, a shaft of moonlight came through the wired-up window. Just then I heard a piercing squeal – a rat. I decided to attack. I stealthily slid from my bunk and reached for the goose gun, feeling the cold metal in the dark. I slipped two BB cartridges into the chambers and slunk like a cat towards the door. I opened it to see several rats playing around the gangplank.

I took careful aim and fired – and missed. I had forgotten that at such close range with choke barrels the shot pattern, though lethal, would be far too narrow for an easy kill.

The dangers of our sport

Careless use of guns inevitably costs lives in the field from time to time. When I was shooting with Kenzie and others our gun safety code was meticulous and over very many years we shot without incident and lived to tell the tale. If you live to a good age, you are enjoying the benefits of shrewd and wise decisions, or you may just have had a charmed life.

Fishing too can be dangerous in rivers, lakes and oceans. Alone on the boat one day, a gale and spring tide threatened to float me out into the

Wash at night with moorings broken. That fired my imagination, as I could have been doomed. You must respect nature, as it will often try to claim your life. There are other fates besides drowning. More than one fisherman has been taken by a crocodile, and in 1984 the wife of a Danish angler fly fishing for trout in Kenya's Aberdare Mountains was killed by a lion.

The call of the wild geese

It was both a seminal and an awesome experience when I pulled out a gosling with the twelve-bore. It was 22nd Sept 1969 at 6.10 in the evening, and the story appeared in *Shooting Times*. Life gives you one chance to do what you love and enjoy, and it is not a rehearsal, it is the real thing.

The sound of wild geese in the estuary is primal and elemental, and thrills you to the bone. You hear the sounds from afar and then the clamour overhead in a moment when they become your world. On the Wash the winds blow in from

Siberia, and at times they will lift you off the sea wall. You come alive in remote wilderness and on the edge of survival, you live on instincts honed from deep within a brain. You know you are one small soul in the great web of vibrant life on earth, and far from the madding crowd of city torment. It is a place where men may become giants of the spirit, alone in the vastness of life.

1970 was the year when I spent my 21st birthday party by myself on Mackenzie Thorpe's houseboat, and met up with a fowler and his son from Rotherham. Geese were flighting in and out of the potato fields while I listened with open ears from the gangplank. There was intense anticipation as I sneaked into a tidal creek by the sluice beyond Shep White's. It was a flight in the twilight, as three geese came in range. Sweeping the gun skyward, I dropped one out onto the sea lavender. Old Kenzie said "Trust you to bag a rarity", for the bird was a yellow-billed bean goose (now a protected species). They may be found in the company of the more common pinkfoot. The party ended in singular satisfaction.

In the Wash estuary some of the marshland birds were difficult quarry, calling for acute senses and sharp shooting. Imagine being alone in murky rain by twilight attempting to bag diminutive jack snipe and golden plover (both protected now) with a 12 bore. You need to be very spry to bring home even a small bag of these fast and canny waders. A right and a left is some result when the odds of cold gloom are stacked against you.

The corollary is that a true wilderness man is alienated by city life. I became an academic who relished wild open places. Many of my sweetest moments have been within the sight and sound of wild birds. I recall a flight of whooper swans, highlighted by sun on grey cloud, and they filled my open eyes with beauty. Later I got Kenzie to depict the scene in oils on canvas. It was real experience I sought, not passive imagery on TV.

Wild geese are embedded in wildfowling folklore. Many rough shooting men will never bag an estuarine pink. The Wash wilderness selects out the case-hardened individuals who will sit out in a frozen tidal creek in a gale full of snowflakes. I still shiver at the memory of an all-night vigil in January with Dave Twedell from ABC College in 1968, when we were young, daft and free. The total bag was two frozen bones.

You will pit all your resolve and exploit all your senses in pursuit of these lovely migrants from Spitzbergen and Greenland. It is most exciting to roast the kill afterwards, as it reflects ancient ritual. Now I reflect in sweet nostalgia on the great eccentrics that have coloured my life, like old Kenzie, Cocker and Shinny. I do like my rugged individualists.

Evening flight

It was a wild and lonely evening flight, with the sea foaming in on a high spring tide. The scudding clouds in a refreshing gale alerted my senses, and

I heard and spotted brent geese, common scoters and the beautiful shelduck. My brain was buzzing with anticipation: this is an experience that only wilderness can create.

As lay in hiding among solid boulders, a big flight of teal emerged from the water flashes to the right. I pulled out three with the right barrel and one with the left as it sprung skyward. I ate all the birds after this intoxicating experience in the remote elements, although the execution of it was clinical. In the wilderness you touch base and find your soul and spirit.

Over the years my spiritual love for the natural world through the ruthless killing spirit was subsumed in a sea of love, compassion and reverence for wonder and beauty. A lovely poem is a far greater achievement than a dead bird. I shot my final old cock pheasant in 1980 in the apple orchard at Sycamore Cottage, Holtby, York. It was stalked with a BSA Airsporter air rifle, and the bird was as tough as teak to eat. The fox I faced gave me feelings for nature which made me into a confirmed conservationist in a psyche negated by guilt of my early plunder.

Pigeon shooting with Kenzie

The humble woodpigeon is found everywhere, and it has great qualities as a sporting bird as well as on the table. It has beauty, cunning and a devastating turn of speed when it needs it and is second only to the curlew in the variety of shots it offers. The curlew of course is now protected, but the pigeon can be shot all the year round. It is unfortunate that the powers that be have recently changed the law on shooting woodpigeons so that you are now allowed to kill them only to protect crops, not for sport or to eat them, despite the fact that these birds are becoming more numerous by the year, so they certainly do not need protection, and of course they are a cheap and tasty source of wild food.

Lincolnshire and Cambridgeshire offer some of the best pigeon shooting in the country. My old pal Shinny and I arranged to go shooting with Kenzie during our summer holidays. Naturally we made the houseboat our HQ, as it was isolated, cheap and could be made comfortable. We looked forward eagerly to our forays with the master. I say 'master' because even in his sixties, Kenzie could wipe pigeon out of the sky as neatly as if they were wiping away with a feather duster. Any pigeon that was unfortunate enough to fly within range was usually a dead one.

Our transport was a 1930s Fiat which was little more than a two-seater glass bubble, but even so it was an improvement on the previous Ford Popular. We collected Kenzie from his home in Sutton Bridge, a journey of some 12 miles along tortuous lanes and dykes from Shep White's. We loaded up the diminutive car with the pigeon gear and I squeezed into the back before we set off on the long drive to Cambridgeshire. Thornley was the destination, and now that name is formally linked with pigeon shooting. On arrival we took a long track which bordered huge fields before stopping and walking along a railway line which flanked a series of dense woods which were obviously the main roosting area. Pigeons were clattering out of every available niche and roosting in the trees or even on the ground.

John Shinn trekked off into the distance to try to find a spinney, while Kenzie put me – the 'Boy' as he always called me – in the thick of the wood. I was feeling a sense of occasion as I bent the natural cover over, ten-foot-high burdocks bearing fruit, to provide concealment, which was soon virtually total.

I crouched down like a dog fox and waited for the birds to flight. They soon came thick and fast, and I was soon shooting constantly. I could do nothing wrong; my confidence ensured my ability to hit the quarry. The first bird arrived at 3pm, and the shooting continued for a further one and a half hours. I was connecting with everything I fired at. Two birds approached side by side, and both fell to my shots. A single bird approached at great speed at the limit of range; I raised the gun and it fell dead to earth.

Unknown to me, Kenzie was watching his young protégé. 'Hell of a shot!' he cried. He came over to collect my bag. 'There must be fifty-five dead pigeons out there,' he declared. Intensely proud, I walked back the 50 yards or so to the railway line. Even here, the track was littered with dead pigeons. 'You're the best young shot on pigeons I've ever had out with me' he said.

I tried to contain my newly-inflated ego as Shinny lumbered up self-consciously from the spinney with a mere three pigeons. He had not shot so well that day.

I was soon brought back down to Planet Earth when I missed a simple shot on the way back to the car. A further hide some yards away brought equal rewards, and pigeons and stock doves were falling to the gun. It was a memorable experience.

Shooting wild

Kenzie and I had another memorable assault on the pigeons when we set off one day to Holbeach St Marks. The site was a bean field, this crop being greatly loved by pigeons, and we had collected a couple of characters from Buxton Gun Club. I had my reservations about their excited boasts about their prowess. I feel a hunter should be like a silent executioner and should preferably operate alone, although naturally a shoot is often a social occasion with friends gathered to shoot together. But I believe the essence of shooting is the lone individual relying on his wits who strikes as efficiently as any natural predator to make his mark on nature.

Once again Kenzie put 'the Boy' in a favourable position, while the other two guns were relegated to the lean side of the field. I was soon shooting strongly as pigeons floated past in droves. The sky was turning steely grey, with the pigeons darker grey against it.

Kenzie was watching again. 'You're shooting well but wild,' he said. Immediately I started to tone down my approach and shoot with more control and deliberation. Good pigeon shooting is about quietly despatching the birds from the air into a well-defined killing zone. There will be an optimum distance at which the experienced gun can kill quickly and efficiently.

We saw the afternoon out kneeling in the mud. The bag was fairly small, about 50 pigeons in all, of which the two 'experts' accounted for about seven. Kenzie was complaining of a painful knee, and it was this injury which years later finally forced him to give up his wildfowling adventures.

Wildfowling with the jet set

I had forgotten the torch, a silly slip as the saltings are harsh and unforgiving. Kenzie had issued the order 'Three-thirty by the little bush' – a daunting prospect.

I opened the houseboat door and stepped off

the gangplank into the night air. It was like walking into a black hole, but the tingle of the marsh wind on my face and the whiff of iodine were intoxicating.

My progress along the sea wall was tortuous, and fear only compounded its difficulty. The creeks leading to the safety of the wall seemed like an SAS assault course. It was best to probe and feel with the toes through your thigh waders while gauging the width and depth of the tidal creeks. I knew I had to protect my gun at all costs. However the difficulty of my passage only heightened perception and increased my desire to meet my guide and mentor by the little bush as arranged. I arrived safely at the sea wall, panting but relieved and proud. How commanding was the darkness and the lunar remoteness of the Wash saltings.

I carried on at a comfortable pace, each step taking me gradually closer to my destination. The red light of the observation tower caught my attention. Further along the sea wall I came to a farmhouse. My eyes and ears were alert for every changing facet of the night scene. The stout supports of the 'dark tower' lingered on; there were few landmarks in this endless horizon. A whistling wind made sounds more audible, like the startled roosting pigeon, quick to leave the safety of its perch and disappear like a passing cloud into the night sky. The few trees, mainly sycamore, were massive, their branches long forced inland by the marsh wind sweeping its way down from the Arctic.

The house appeared dark and threatening in my young mind and I imagined it to be some medieval relic, the haunt of some ancient demon. I did not dare to tread down in the shadows where the sea wall dropped down to it. I glanced warily behind to make sure I was alone.

In the distance I spotted a faint light moving rhythmically. It was Kenzie, and I had found the bush, a shrubby little hawthorn and our signpost to the way to deep and fruitful creeks.

Kenzie muttered a gruff 'Morning'. I was not

pleased to see that with him were two more wildfowlers, smartly-dressed middle-class types. 'We've just come from the bridge at a hundred miles an hour in an E-type,' Kenzie told me. They looked like townie jet-setters to me, overdressed in tweeds and overequipped.

I was excited, yet I remained self-possessed as we struck off over the marsh. We followed the line of some good flat marsh used for grazing along the false bank and took our stations along a nice shell-bottomed creek. I settled into a comfortable position to await the expected, or the unexpected. A Second World War walkie-talkie carrier proved ideal for use both as a pillow and a haversack. You could shoot seated, kneeling or lying back for the most difficult shots. In the vast open spaces of the saltings visibility is crucial, while not to be seen yourself is imperative. In those days the quarry could be godwit, curlew, golden plover or grey plover as well as duck and geese.

Dawn that morning would come at about 6 am. It would be a long wait, so a clear mind would be essential. The cold and discomfort heightened our alertness and helped us to resist drowsiness and torpor.

The spring tide started to creep its way through the myriad creeks, and soon swirls of water were appearing. Waders in their thousands could be heard bubbling away in their gregarious and often hysterical fashion. The sharp, eerie cries of curlew were audible; they would soon flight to higher marshes and their dawn feeding on the great grasslands.

Several godwit flew by in the half-light – legal quarry back then – but they were out of range. I heard no shots. Perhaps this would be a blank night.

Then I heard the clear trill of a curlew. I shrank back into cover in case the bird came within range of the full-choke barrel. I heard Kenzie call to the bird, which momentarily veered into the wind in response and promptly fell to his shot.

No more shots were fired that morning. Back at the sea wall, Kenzie remarked laconically, 'We've done well, one call, one shot, and that's how it should be done'. It was a lesson to the E-Type pair, who had no doubt expected a mass slaughter of the wildfowl population of the marshes. We separated and Kenzie began the walk back, to return later with more eager clients, while I began the long trek back to his houseboat.

Lost in the fog

The Wash wildfowler must treat discipline as his watchword. The marsh can be unpredictable, and it can claim the life of the innocent or unwary. Man is the interloper here, and this flat wilderness can do fine without us. It is all too easy, through over-excitement, fear or stupidity, to fall foul of this inhospitable place. As a young man I was foolhardy and unyielding, even when the bounds of caution had been reached.

I was out one early morning when it was slightly foggy. Despite this I had planned a morning flight, hopefully at the geese. I trekked out to the stalk edges and found a nice creek, good and deep but narrow enough for concealment. The atmosphere was still and heavy with damp and the darkness was impenetrable. It was a lonely, lonely place. What's more, eerie wisps of fog were now starting to form. These soon joined up to form banks of fog which were so dense that I knew all chances of a goose had gone. I knew I would now have to return to the safety of the houseboat before the conditions deteriorated any further.

I looked around for a marker or reference point, but nothing was visible. Fear began to creep upon me, and I was beginning to feel hot under my Solway zipper and with all my gear. At first I staggered around in all directions trying to find a recognisable creek or channel, but it was impossible to see anything. I had made the mistake of not bringing a compass – I had always felt they were for nancies.

Suddenly a familiar noise pierced the fog – the sound of a car passing on the other side of the sea wall. Thank god for that, I grunted to myself. Now I knew which way I had to go. I plunged off into the void, panting and with heart thumping. But as I floundered across the marsh the mud seemed to get softer and deeper, and worse, the tide was rising and filling the creeks around me, and I could smell kelp. Then I heard the sound again from in front of me – but now I knew it was not a car at all. It was the foghorn of a ship out on the North Sea. I was going the wrong way and charging towards danger.

I turned around and floundered back away from the sound, to reach the safety of the sea wall at last. How easily I could have died that morning out on the marsh, trapped by mud and a rushing tide.

Dogs, Our
Hunting Companions

Boxing Day

Yesterday when I was young and felt so strong

I was out with dog and gun

Under an ice crystal sun

Beyond the shroud, the foreboding crowd

*I dwelt in hedgerows, barley stubble and
meadows*

*Where rabbits lived and pheasants hid to escape
the lonely hunter.*

*I came alive on the earthy clod and felt the power
of the cosmic flow*

That coursed energy from deep below.

*It is good to tap the primal self that fuels the
mind with the oxygen of insight.*

And now alone in the rain-sodden gloom

I recall when my youth was in full bloom.

Hunting with dogs

Hunting with dogs is a traditional sport in the UK and on a global level. The wildest dogs I have seen, with great pack instincts, are African hunting dogs. All our dogs are descendants of Lupus the wolf, to refer to that marvellous novel by Jack London *The Call of the Wild*. A timber wolf in full cry under the moonlight is my favourite animal. It is the very call of the wild, and the wolf is a rugged, instinctual and most intelligent creature.

Dogs have been my companions through many of my own adventures in the wild. My first was a fine black Labrador called Ben, a lovely, brave old dog, which I acquired in 1865 when I was 16. As a puppy he spent the first night in bed with me to socialise him. His initial training was done by a keeper who knew his dogs. With my Acme whistles and staghorn stop whistle I would learn to control him, and he became a loyal and obedient and special friend. Ben happily swam dykes, climbed bushes and jumped barbed wire fences to retrieve hares, rabbits and assorted game. He was a grand dog. Ben was a lovely, brave old dog. I well remember the day a single woodie appeared at long range and I took it in a very sporting shot. 'Hi Lost', and the dog raced off to retrieve the single pigeon. Ages came and went by with no sight of Ben. When I went to investigate, I found him straddling dense bramble bushes and attempting to climb up to the fork of a hawthorn tree.

We went rough shooting and occasional wildfowling at Kenzie's for the next couple of years, but when I went to college in 1967 it put a temporary halt to my roller pigeons and my time with Ben. Formal academic influence would take over the next 10 years – I have yet to recover from the brainwashing.

In later years Dad took Ben to the office each day. What a lovely game dog he was. It was a sad day when I buried him under the old apple trees at Sycamore Cottage, Holtby, in 1980.

I have loved my chats with terrier and lurcher people and have seen some great dogs out there, from hard-bitten terriers to elegant and graceful lurchers. We become fond of our furry friends, and I loved all my dogs for their spirit, instinct and purpose. My mother always said that the animal kingdom was far superior to the human one – there is wisdom in that dictum. She was a gem with birds and animals.

A dog to fill a hole

In 1985 Freddie the Jack Russell was born on a farm at Lower Marishes in Yorkshire. Freddie, who belonged to my wife Jean's mother, was a canny dog and could interpret in his canine way what I was thinking. I loved that dog, and as I write a tear forms in my eye. He was an expert footballer, and his claim to fame was climbing up to the cottage roof on the clematis. When I pulled him down, there was a fat rat in his mouth.

When Freddie died Jean's mum was lonely. I knew a coursing greyhound man from Rufforth called Ray Wilson, who said he had a nice little retired bitch of Irish origin called Lady Jane Cooneen. With great anticipation Jean and I went to collect her. A huge, athletic dog bounded up the paddock to greet us. Then Ray introduced us to this beautiful tiger-stripe bitch. Thanks to bad teeth, her breath really ponged. Off we shot in the Clio van to show Jean's mum, who was shocked by her size. We left the old lady open-mouthed with her new love.

We did have a hilarious experience when the poor old lady panicked because the dog had apparently vanished, only to be found stuck fast behind the settee. A lovely quiet animal was that old dog. She would take a rabbit on the lead with one snap of her jaws as we were walking along Holtby lane. She won more than 12 firsts and became the spiritual companion of my mother until she was 92. Jean's mother's dying words to me were 'Look after Jane'.

Sadly all the great dogs go the way of all flesh in the end, but Jane lived on until she was 13 years old.

Hunting with dogs

Man has relied on the superior speed, cunning and sense of smell of dogs to help him in his hunting since time immemorial. Wild dogs are superb hunters, using their intelligence to work as a pack and so bring down vastly bigger animals than themselves. African hunting dogs sustain great speed and stamina, as do the lovely dingos of Australia. A wild dog knows more than man can dream of; raw nature is truly wonderful. The scientists have confirmed that all our domestic dogs are bred down from Lupus the wolf, which remains a ruthless wild killing machine, having survived the persecution of man.

Hunting with dogs is a traditional sport in the UK as it is in most countries of the world, but the wildest dogs I have seen, with great pack instincts, are African hunting dogs. All our dogs are descendants of Lupus the wolf, and a timber wolf in full cry under the moonlight is my favourite animal. It is the epitome, the very call of the wild, for the wolf is a rugged, instinctual and most intelligent creature.

Ratting with hardnosed terriers is both lethal and exciting – the dogs go into a little frenzy and the rats squeak in terror. Before hare coursing was banned I used to go along with the Old Yorkshire Coursing Club. There were some clever dogs to see in full gallop, yet many of the fit, fly and strong hares escaped. Many of the old traditions continue under cover, although banned by law.

I do feel that man could be perceived as cruel in manipulating, exploiting and preying on birds and animals. In common with many men as they grow older, I no longer, hunt, fish or shoot on compassionate grounds, and because my feelings towards nature. However men will always desire to hunt as a primal and instinctual response to a natural urge bred in us in the days when we were primitive creatures who relied on our hunting skills for the survival of ourselves and our families.

Man and Nature

The Doors of Perception

Open the doors, peel back the mind
Unleash the senses to the outer world
Do you see what I see, everyday reality,
Or are we all souls in a world of flux?
Probe deep;
Search for the inner and outer realms
Layers of meaning can be perceived
Who's to say what is real and what is surreal?

Our place in the natural world

'Far from the madding crowd' has been the mantra for my great years spent in mountains, woods, deserts and seas as far away as the Sahara and the roof of the world in the Himalaya. The process starts with home socialisation by parents, rural studies and ecology, and countryside management should be a compulsory part of the school curriculum. Materialism and capitalism have warped the perceptions and values of millions of people who need to take a walk on the wild side and bask in the spirit of nature, to sense it and feel it at a primordial level of being.

As living beings, humanity shares the planet with a myriad other lifeforms. In the grand scale of the cosmos they can be perceived as one united entity of life on Planet Earth. Each creature has a role to play, and is significant in the total web of earthly existence. I believe we have an individual responsibility to nurture and treasure the vast yet declining living resources we share with countless species, from the tiniest microbe to the largest elephant. The practical essence will be understanding of conservation needs on a global level. I would like to see a rise in spiritual beliefs from within, and generated by nature, and active education of the naïve and greedy to reverse the trends of environmental pollution. The ideals are lofty and transcendent, yet the practical needs in reality are onerous and pressing.

I believe we have an ethical duty to promote and conserve all life forms, not just man. Billions need to be spent on ecologically sound farming practices and educating people of all walks of life about our heritage, which is the wonder and beauty of the species we may hunt and share Planet Earth with.

Genius and madness

We are all here for society to make vital judgements on us with the language and thought of the day. I believe that if you sit in a creek all night in January waiting for ducks and geese with fingers frozen to the gun barrels, then you qualify to be called a little mad (or a lot). I did many such things in my 'hard' wildfowling days. I always believed in mind over matter. Today the snow is on the ground as I reflect on genius and madness. Similarly with pigeon shooting, waiting in a north-east wind for birds to fly from Barcelona into Yorkshire is assisted by a little madness. If you stretch your mind to the limit, it will definitely make you psychotic.

Out in raw nature, keen observation is key to a profound perception of reality. My mind understands it as a Zen-like awareness and mindfulness. How you perceive this depends on how your brain functions and suits introverts best, I think. In my life I have been labelled both mad and psychotic, but at the end of the day we are what we are. Genius and madness then are just words to try to describe the undesirable.

I admire the TV presenter Chris Packham's eye for detail; he has admitted to having Asperger's syndrome, a mild form of autism. The suave, charming, extroverted narrations of David Attenborough are worldly in their global enthusiasm. Both have a fanatical love of expressing personality in relation to the natural world and both are clever and interesting men.

Humanity does flush out some luminaries, such as Jacob Bronowski, who manifested the more positive aspects of the natural sciences suffused by philosophy. The power of these eloquent individuals may have great impact on the popular consciousness of the day via the written word and film. However beyond collective knowledge is the original insight peculiar to me, and I touch on this reservoir in my writing.

The wonders of the Earth

Many years ago I made a conscious decision to escape the rigours of the rat race. In reality we are all isolates, little islands in the stream. I shy away from objectivity and harsh external reality. The concrete jungle is a painful experience for my personal sensibilities, and I find solace in my beautiful world of poetry and philosophical abstraction. It is my little microcosm within the macrocosm, and it feels right for me.

I believe my creative writing lays down a record of a subjective world, expressing originality in an introverted way. With six books out there now for all to read, I hope I will make some impact on the popular consciousness.

The impact of man on the natural world is enormous, resulting in many endangered species, much habitat despoliation and destruction and huge effects on global ecosystems. Yet we can flow along with and help nature in so many ways. With the expansion of materialism, rising human population levels, changes in habitat and natural selection, I fear for the future of many peoples and many of the other lifeforms on the earth. You must consider your own personal perception of your responsibilities to the great outdoors, a place that I love.